T0378676

GET OUT ALIVE!

ESCAPE FROM THE ICE PROWLER

CHERRY LAKE PRESS

Published in the United States of America by Cherry Lake Publishing Group
Ann Arbor, Michigan
www.cherrylakepublishing.com

Reading Adviser: Beth Walker Gambro, MS, Ed., Reading Consultant, Yorkville, IL

Photo Credits:
© Igor Kovalchuk/Shutterstock, cover, contents page (polar bear), © Jo Crebbin/Shutterstock cover (seal) and seal page 11, © klyaksun/Shutterstock (graphic on cover and throughout book); © Cassette Bleue/Shutterstock, speech bubbles throughout; © Nazarkru/Shutterstock, yellow bursts throughout; © Peter Hermes Furian/Shutterstock (map), © Alexey Seafarer/Shutterstock (bear) page 4 and bears page 10; © Jan Miko/Shutterstock (top) page 5 and in background throughout book, © Reehan Raza/ Shutterstock, page 5; © Galina Savina/Shutterstock page 6; © KARI K/Shutterstock page 7; © imageBROKER.com/ Shutterstock page 8; © outdoorsman/Shutterstock (top), © Ondrej Prosicky/Shutterstock page 9; © GTW/ Shutterstock (bottom) page 11 and page 21 (bottom); © Fon Duangkamon/Shutterstock page 12; © Sandra Ophorst/Shutterstock page 13; © Monyicola/Shutterstock (top), © NOAA/Michael Cameron page 14; © polarman/Shutterstock page 15; © Nick Pecker/Shutterstock page 16; © Jonas Gruhlke/Shutterstock (top), © Henrik Winther Andersen/Shutterstock page 17; © FloridaStock/Shutterstock page 18, page 22 (top), page 23 (top); © 1410823019/Shutterstock page 19; © wildestanimal/Shutterstock page 20; © Michael Cola/ Shutterstock (top) page 21; © Green Mountain Exposure/Shutterstock (bottom) page 22; © Nirut Sampan/ Shutterstock (bottom) page 23.

Produced for Cherry Lake Publishing by bluedooreducation.com

Library of Congress Cataloging-in-Publication Data has been filed and is available at catalog.loc.gov.

Printed in the United States of America

Note from Publisher: Websites change regularly, and their future contents are outside of our control. Supervise children when conducting any recommended online searches for extended learning opportunities.

ABOUT THE AUTHOR

Julie K. Lundgren grew up in northern Minnesota near Lake Superior. She delighted in picking berries, finding cool rocks, and trekking in the woods. She still does! Julie's interest in nature science led her to a degree in biology. She adores her family, her sweet cat, and Adventure Days.

Contents

GREAT SEA BEAR

At the top of the Earth live fierce **polar** bears. These **marine** animals rule the polar ice of the Arctic Sea area.

"POLAR" REFERS TO BOTH THE NORTH AND SOUTH POLES. "ARCTIC" MEANS ONLY THE FAR NORTH.

I prowl for prey on sea ice during Arctic winters.

During Arctic winter, there is almost no sunlight so far north. The long polar night lasts from about November to January.

Polar bears are fit for life on the ice. A layer of fat protects their bodies. Thick fur wraps them like a cozy blanket.

BUMPY SKIN PADS ON THEIR PAWS HELP GRIP THE ICE.

POLAR BEAR FUR IS ALMOST INVISIBLE IN THE SNOW.

SHARP TEETH AND CLAWS TEAR THROUGH TOUGH SEAL SKIN.

Polar bears hunt two ways. In **still hunting**, they wait by cracks or holes in the ice for seals to pop up to breathe.

If a seal pops up, I will bite its head and drag it out of the water.

In **stealth hunting**, they sniff out seals sheltering in snow and ice dens. If they spot a seal resting on the ice, they may sneak up to it underwater.

SUPER SWIMMER

Arctic ringed seals live in the same areas as polar bears. Their fur **pelts** have ring shapes that look like bubbles. They have pale, roly-poly bellies.

LIKE POLAR BEARS, SEALS NEED FAT TO SURVIVE THE ARCTIC COLD.

Like most seals, Arctic ringed seals have ear holes. They do not have **external** ear flaps.

EAR HOLE

WHISKERS

Did you know seals are **carnivores**? They use their whiskers to sense fish and shrimp moving nearby.

My front flippers help me swim and dig.

SEALS NEED TO BREATHE AIR. IN THE OCEAN, THEY CAN CLAW THROUGH THICK SEA ICE TO MAKE BREATHING HOLES.

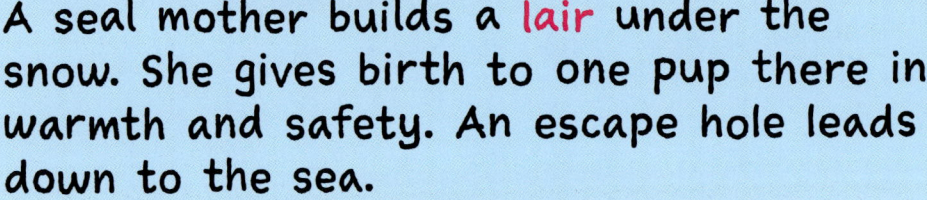

A seal mother builds a lair under the snow. She gives birth to one pup there in warmth and safety. An escape hole leads down to the sea.

At about a month, seal pups shed their white coats for darker adult fur.

A SEAL PUP CAN SWIM WELL AT 3 TO 4 WEEKS OLD.

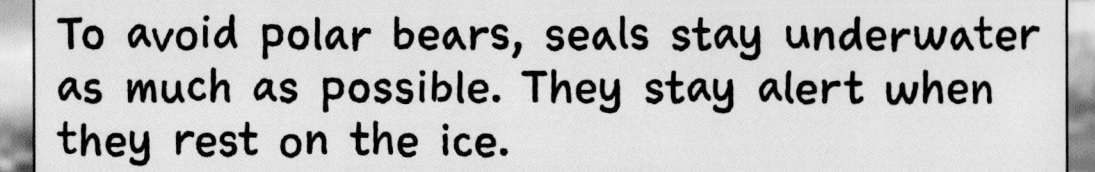

To avoid polar bears, seals stay underwater as much as possible. They stay alert when they rest on the ice.

I rest near cracks in the ice or a breathing hole for quick escapes.

When rising to breathe, ringed seals blow bubbles to test for waiting polar bears.

SEALS HOLD THEIR BREATH UNDER WATER UP TO 45 MINUTES. MOST HUMANS CAN HOLD THEIR BREATH FOR LESS THAN 1 MINUTE!

The bubbles look like seal fur. Polar bears may attack the bubbles and miss the seal.

POLAR STAKEOUT!

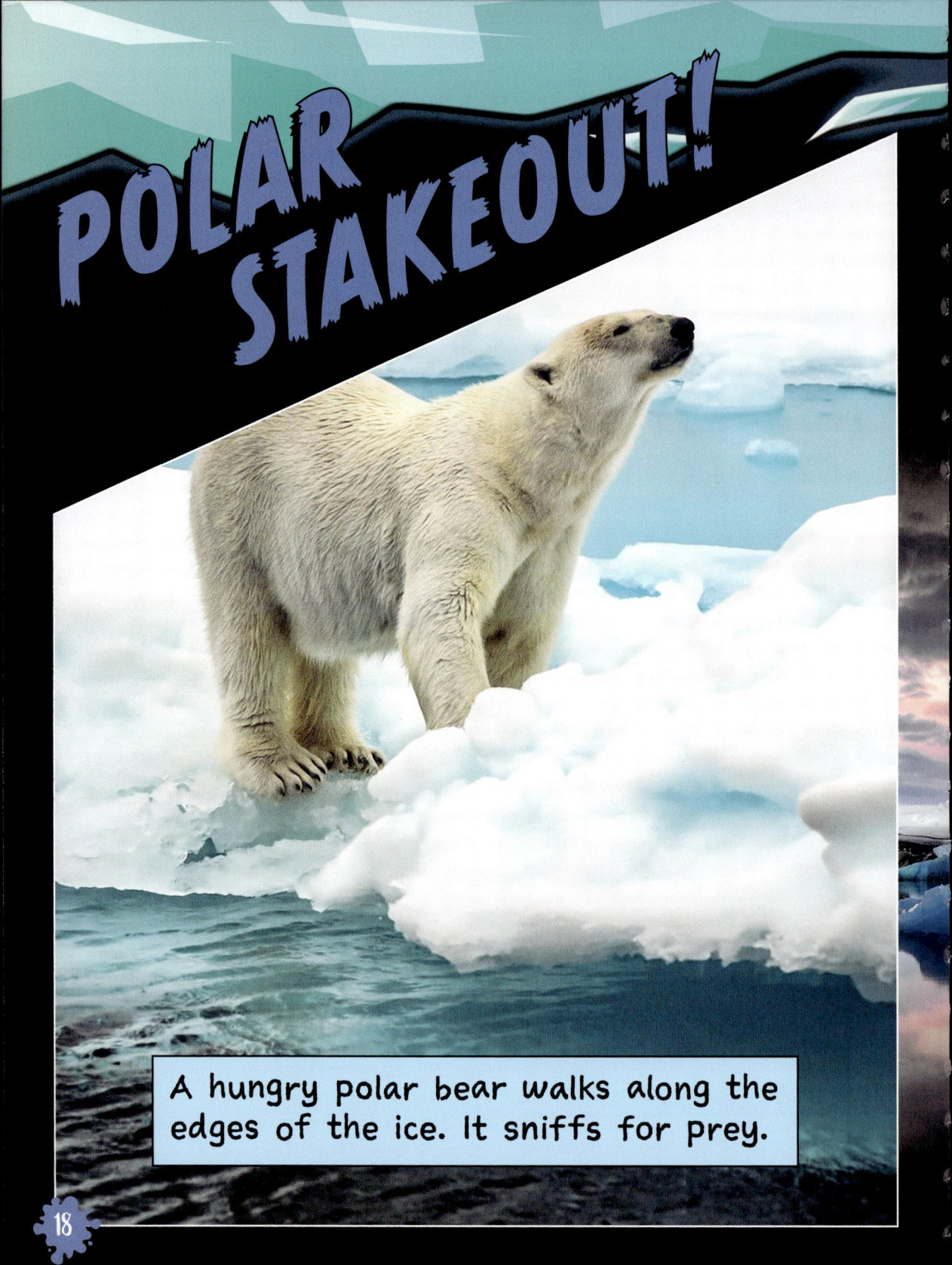

A hungry polar bear walks along the edges of the ice. It sniffs for prey.

Stakeouts take less energy than searching for resting seals.

POLAR BEARS CAN WAIT SILENTLY WITHOUT MOVING FOR HOURS.

19

GET OUT ALIVE!

After still hunting for an hour, the bear sees bubbles rising. High alert!

The bear plunges its head into the sea with jaws snapping.

No seal. Only a mouthful of its bubbles.

The hungry bear is on the prowl again.

The bear listens and sniffs for a seal lair. There! The bear follows the smell of seal to the snowy hideout.

The bear pounces on the lair's roof to find its meal. Deep snow makes the roof hard to break. It gives the seals time to escape down the ice hole.

The bear sniffs for a pup hidden in the crushed lair. No pup! Better luck next time, bear!

Find Out More

Books

Pettiford, Rebecca. *Polar Bears*, Minnetonka, MN: Bellwether Media, 2019

Ryndak, Rob. *Seal or Sea Lion?*, New York, NY: Gareth Stevens Publishing, 2016

Websites

Search these online sources with an adult:

Polar bears | National Geographic Kids

Arctic ringed seals | Britannica

Glossary

carnivores (KAR-nuh-vorz) animals that eat other animals

external (ek-STUR-nuhl) on the outside of something

lair (LAIR) a seal home that is like a snow cave on top of the ice

marine (muh-REEN) in and around the sea, and dependent on it for life

pelts (PELTS) thick fur coats that protect from cold and water

polar (POH-ler) being in a place on or around the North or South Pole

prey (PRAY) animals that are hunted and eaten by other animals

stakeouts (STAYK-owts) time spent waiting to ambush prey

stealth hunting (STELTH HUN-ting) sneaking up on prey

still hunting (STIL HUN-ting) waiting silently without moving until prey is very close

Index